Canning for Beginners

How to Can Vegetables, Fruits, Meats and Fish at Home

Melanie Bennet

clarifying purposes only and are owned by the owners themselves, not affiliated with this document.

Table of Contents

Introduction

Whether you're trying to re-create the old days or want to enjoy healthy food from your own hands, canning is a new skill that you'll love. It's possible to can nearly any type of food. Fruits, vegetables, jams, and even meats can be preserved and canned for consumption later. Some people do canning as a hobby because it's a creative and fun way to learn something new and preserve food. Others can for health reasons because it's a great way to keep nutritious food in your pantry for months. It's also economical; people like to can because it allows them to use all the food they grow, produce, and buy.

There are several reasons why fresh food gets spoiled:
- loss of moisture
- reacting with oxygen
- enzyme activities
- growth of yeast, mold, bacteria, and other microorganisms

The canning process involves placing food in clean containers and heating the food to destroy enzymes and microorganisms that cause food spoilage. The process of heating also drives the air out of the containers. This is why canned food can be kept for long periods.

In this book, we will go through all the basics of canning. From what you need, the different types of canning methods, and delicious canning recipes, you will learn everything you need to start canning foods at home. With that being said... let's get canning!

CHAPTER ONE

Introduction of Canning

If you are a gardener or just love stockpiling ingredients, consider canning your food. This fun hobby is a fantastic pastime for those who like to cook, as it allows you to store up a bounty of delicious produce, meats, broth, and other foods to enjoy throughout the entire year. No experience? No problem! Canning is an easy process that anyone can learn.

What Is Canning?

At its most simple dictionary definition, canning is preserving food in a can. Before modern refrigeration and the invention of bulk grocery stores, families fed themselves through cold winters and unproductive harvests by relying on a pantry filled with canned goods that they produced themselves. The process of canning has not changed much since those days. Most food is stored in either pint or quart-sized jars, although other sizes are also available. To can effectively, you need to use very high heat to preserve food in containers so that microorganisms and harmful bacteria are killed. The canning process removes oxygen from the container, which preserves the food and prevents it from rotting.

There are two ways to do your canning. You can use fresh foods that are not cooked but packed in their raw form into jars and then processed. Or, you can complete this process by cooking the food first and then putting it into jars.

The Benefits of Canning

Canning has many benefits that are good for your health, the environment, your overall wellness, and your bottom line.

It's a healthy method to preserve food
Canned food is better for you than much of the stuff you buy in grocery stores. Like most people, you probably have concerns about pesticides, chemicals, and other toxins in your commercial food. Store-bought canned goods tend to contain high levels of sodium, BPA, and other preservatives. When you can your own food, you know exactly how it is produced from start to finish, and you don't have to wonder how far it traveled to get to your kitchen or what mystery ingredients might be included in it.

It tastes great!
You can't deny the fact that homemade food tastes great. The food you create yourself will taste fresher and more delicious than what you buy in the store. A jar of jam that you canned from the fruit that came off your trees will be sweeter and more enjoyable than a jar processed in a factory.

Creating your own canned food using locally-grown, fresh ingredients gives you scrumptious food that you can readily access whenever you want. And the best part is that you can create different kinds of canned products using recipes or by creating your own experimental food combinations.

It's economical
You will be able to cut your grocery bill down by quite a bit when you don't have to buy things like applesauce, pickles, jams, tomato sauce, veggies, and other foods that you canned when you had the opportunity. You won't have to feel guilty about wasting food because you're using all of it and saving money while you do that. The jars you use are reusable and worthy of the minor investment

you'll have to make in them. Best yet, homemade canned goods make great gifts!

It's eco-friendly too
You will also have a minimal environmental impact when canning your food, as you can reuse the jars instead of throwing them out. This is especially true if you grow your foods, too. By doing this, you remove yourself from the food industry that involves shipping, factory processing, distribution, packaging, and so on.

If you grow your own food or buy it at a local farmer's market, you're placing a lot of value on the local economy and the land in your community. You'll find a lot of personal satisfaction in the environmental element and your natural abilities to prepare food for the long term and feed your family.

This chapter shows you what canning is and why you should do it. If you're ready to get started, your next steps are to learn how to successfully can your food and what you'll need to do to get started. You'll find the canning process to be healthy, satisfying, and a lot of fun.

CHAPTER TWO

How To Can Your Foods at Home

Canning your own food is healthy, economical, and great for the environment. Knowing how to can your foods will leave you feeling self-reliant and positive about what you're putting into your body. There won't be any wondering about the chemicals and preservatives that have been stuffed into the food you bring home from the grocery store.

As you prepare to learn the process of canning, remember that mistakes will be made, and that's okay. Learn from them, go back to the beginning, and start again. These are some brief instructions on how to can your foods so you can begin trying it right away. Gather all those fruits and veggies from your garden or the leftovers you picked out at the farmer's market, and get to work.

Preparations

You can spend money on the latest and greatest canning gadgets. Prices range from $25 to over $500 for in-home canning systems that include a pressurizer that allows you to prepare canned foods instantly and efficiently. If you want to invest in this type of operation, go for it. However, it's not necessary. You can set up a canning system that closely resembles the way homesteaders and pioneers canned their food ages ago. You only need a few things. If your canning really takes off and becomes a serious part of your life, you can consider buying a pressure canner. But–you don't have to when you're getting started.

Jars

The most important pieces of equipment you'll want to have in your kitchen are your jars. Most people use Ball jars or Mason jars, and as long as it's glass, durable, and clear, you should have excellent results. There are so many sizes, shapes, and types of jars available that you can quickly become overwhelmed. There are even decorative canning jars available for when you want to give away your creations as gifts. That's an exciting prospect, but keep it simple as you learn how to can your own foods.

Start with some high-quality jars of various sizes. When you're following a specific canning recipe, you'll probably have instructions on what size jar to use. It's a good idea to stock different sizes, so you're ready for what you want to can. When you're choosing sizes, think about how your jars will fit in your cupboards, refrigerator, and freezer.

Something else to consider with your jars is mouth size. That's the size of the opening at the top of the jar. It may not matter how wide that mouth is when you're canning things like jams, jellies, and sauces, but when you need to load large chunks of fruits, vegetables, and other larger foods into your jars, a wider mouth will make a difference.

Jar Lids and Bands

Lids and bands are additional important pieces of equipment. They must fit the jars, obviously, and usually, you can buy the lid and jar together. However, you'll only use the lid one time, so you'll need a supply of extra lids. When you're shopping, make sure the lids are BPA-free. You're looking for lids that will be airtight and good at forming a seal. You may find plastic lids available, with advertising that assures you they are reusable. However, the only USDA-approved canning lids are metal coated and designed to be used only one time.

Pots

Another inexpensive piece of equipment that will be required for your canning purposes is a large pot. Your pot will need to be big enough to hold water that will cover your jars and still leave a little room at the top. You will be boiling water, so be generous with the pot size. You don't want to have scalding water spraying down your kitchen. A stockpot usually works, and stick with something nonreactive. Stainless steel stockpots are your best options, and enamel-coated iron is also good.

Jar Lifters

While jar lifters might seem like an unnecessary accessory, they can be quite useful in your canning process. They are also inexpensive. You can find a great pair of jar lifters for less than $10, and you will be thrilled to have them. You'll get a better grip on the jars as you pull them out of boiling water.

Canning Ladle

While this tool isn't really "essential," it will allow you to fill your canning jars faster than a traditional kitchen ladle.

Steam Pressure Canner

This is a requirement when you can foods using the steam pressure canning method—mainly for low-acid foods. Make sure you have your steam pressure canner tested every 3 years or so to ensure that it's still working well.

Canning Methods

There are two main methods for canning; water bath canning and pressure canning. Either type of canner is typically made out of steel, stainless steel, aluminum, and porcelain.

Water bath canners are the easiest to use and least expensive varieties but can only safely process foods that are considered high-acidity. Foods that are safe for a water bath system include fruits, pickled items, and tomatoes (with added salt). Water bath canners are simple, requiring you to submerge jars in boiling water for a set period of time. When you remove them and allow them to cool, the lids of the jars form an airtight seal that prevents bacteria from entering. Most water bath canners cost less than $50.

Pressure canners are more expensive and slightly more complicated but can process all of the same foods as a water bath canner, plus all other vegetables, broths, and meats. Pressure canning demands more attention than water bath canning.

Pressure canners increase the temperature of your jars to temperatures hotter than boiling through the use of confined pressure. This helps eliminate the risk of botulism, which is a serious infection caused by bacterial spores. These are most commonly found in foods low in acid, as are issues such as mold and other growths. Pressure canners usually cost between $100 and $200.

Water Bath Canning

Prepare Everything

First, make sure your jars, lids, and bands work before using them. Don't use jars that are chipped, scratched, or compromised. You don't want them to break during the canning process. Wash your jars, lids, and bands in warm water with soap, and dry them. Here are some tips for you when preparing (sterilizing) the canning jars:

- Fill a stockpot or canner with water at least halfway to the top. The water should be enough to completely cover the jars with at least 1 inch of water above them.
- Bring the water to a rolling boil before adding the jars.
- Use a pair of tongs to add the canning jars, seals, and lids separately.
- Leave each of the items completely submerged in the boiling water for a minimum of 5 minutes. Check to make sure that the seals don't stick together.
- After sterilization, place the items on a clean cloth or wooden surface.

Part of the preparation process is preparing the food. This process will depend on the canning recipe. Make sure to prepare the food items as indicated, so the food items get preserved in the best way possible.

Fill the Jars

After sterilizing your canning jars, you can start using them. One important thing to note is that you have to sterilize all canning jars, even those you haven't used yet. Just because they came from the store and are new doesn't mean that they are already sterile and clean enough for use. After sterilizing your jars and preparing the food as per the recipe, here are some steps for filling the jars:

- Gently pour the prepared food, liquid, or sauce into the jars. Use a funnel to make this easier, and make sure that you leave at least ½-inch of headspace at the top of the jar. The funnel, spoon, and any other tools you use to pour the food into the jars should be as sterile as the jars themselves.
- Use a bubble remover to remove any air bubbles by sliding the tool between the food and the jar. You can also use chopsticks, a rubber spatula, or any other similar tool for this task.
- Use a clean, damp cloth to wipe the rims of the jars clean.
- Place the lids on the jars, then screw the bands until finger-tight. Check the seals of the jars by pressing down on the tops of the lids. You know it's okay when the lids don't move.

Process the Jars

After filling the jars and sealing them, it's time to process. This is the most important step in the process because it completely sterilizes the jars and the contents inside. Processing involves heating the jars and the contents. Important as this step is, it's not necessary for canning some types of foods like freshly pickled veggies. For such food items, you must place the jars in the refrigerator right after you seal them. This reduces the contamination risk. Usually, the recipe will indicate whether you have to process the jars or not. If the recipe calls for processing, here are some basic steps for you to follow:

- Use the same stockpot you used to sterilize the empty jars.
- Add enough water to cover the jars completely in at least 1

inch of water. Preheat this water to 140 degrees for raw-packed foods and 180 degrees for hot-packed foods.

- Place the jars inside the stockpot using a jar lifter. When placing the jars, make sure there is a 2-inch gap between them. If needed, process the jars in batches. If they tend to move around, or if you are processing with a half-full canner, place some clean rags between them to prevent the jars from breaking. Add more water if there is no longer an inch above the jars. Also, don't place the jars directly at the bottom of the pot, as they may break. Place a rack at the bottom for the jars to sit on while processing them.

- Place a lid on the stockpot and allow the water to return to a rolling boil. Set a timer and allow the water to continue to boil for as long as your recipe requires. Most recipes require at least fifteen minutes of processing time. Once the time has elapsed, take the canner off the burner and remove the lid.

- Wait a few minutes, and then use a jar lifter to extract the jars. Place them on a clean towel or wooden surface to cool.

Check the Jars

It's best to allow the jars to cool and rest completely, at least for a day. As your jars cool, they may make popping sounds. Then the next thing to do is check the seals to make sure that they didn't break during processing. Press down on the top of each lid to check the seals. If you discover that any of the jars have broken seals, discard the contents. It may seem like a waste to discard the food, but it's better than eating something that might make you sick. You can reuse the jar after throwing out the contents. Just make sure to sterilize the jars again to prepare them for the next batch of food.

As for reusing the lid, that depends on the type of lid you use. If you have a basic metal lid with a rubber gasket, you can't use it again. The main reason is that the rubber gasket usually gets deformed after processing. Thus, you can't reuse it for your next batch of canned food. However, there are reusable canning lids that come with a separate ring gasket. But these lids may lead to seal failure, so you have to double- and even triple-check them before storing. Because of the unreliable nature of reused lids, it's recommended to opt for single-use lids for canning.

High-acid foods
Water bath canning is recommended for high-acid foods. Most types of fruits are high in acid. Pickled veggies and fermented foods are also considered high-acid foods. Some examples of high-acid food items are:

- Apples
- Applesauce
- Apricots
- Berries
- Cherries
- Chutney
- Grapes
- Fruit jams
- Fruit jellies
- Fruit pie fillings
- Nectarines
- Peaches
- Pears
- Peppers
- Pickled vegetables
- Plums
- Relish
- Salsa
- Sauerkraut
- Tomatoes

Pressure Canning

When you want to can low-acidic foods like meats, seafood, and most vegetables, use a pressure canner. You're following the same process, but the level of heat is far more extreme to protect the flavor and safety.

Pressure canners received a bad rap for many years, as there were several reports of exploding pressure canners that caused severe injuries. However, newer models are incredibly safe, and issues only tend to arise when you try to build your own pressure canner. Avoid this by investing in a quality pressure canner and paying close attention to the canner while processing your food.

Pressure canners are divided into several key parts, including pressure gauges, gaskets, safety fuses, racks, and automatic vents. To start, fill the canner with water in exactly the same way you would as preparing a water bath. Again, prep your jars and fill the canner once the water is ready.

When you are ready to process the jars, you must heat the canner to the highest possible temperature, allowing steam to escape from the vent for several minutes. Then, close the vent and allow the canner to become pressurized. You must closely watch the gauge on your canner to wait for it to reach the ideal pressure for your recipe. Once the ideal pressure is reached, you must adjust the heat to make sure the canner maintains a consistent pressure. If it does not stay at the proper pressure, you could contaminate your food.

When the set amount of time has elapsed, you can turn off the heat. Do not remove the canner lid until the pressure has dropped back down—this can cause steam burns and other injuries, as well as food spoilage. Let the canner cool for about an hour before removing the lid. Then, extract, cool, and store your jars in the same method as you would for a water bath system.

Low-acid foods

These include meats and most types of vegetables. These foods don't have enough acidity to prevent the growth of spores and bacteria that remains after exposure to boiling water. In particular, the bacterium *clostridium botulinum* can cause food poisoning. This is why the pressure canning method is recommended for such foods since it involves higher temperatures. Some examples of low-acid food items are:

- Asparagus
- Beef
- Beets
- Carrots
- Dried beans
- Green beans
- Okra
- Peas

- Peppers
- Potatoes
- Poultry
- Pumpkin
- Seafood
- Soups
- Stews
- Sweet corn
- Meat sauces
- Mincemeat pie filling
- Wild game

Safety

When it comes to cooking and preparing any kind of food, safety should be your number one priority. You don't want to eat something that will make you sick, and you don't want to share something with your loved ones that will make them sick. To reduce your risk of ending up with spoiled canned food, here are some things to keep in mind:

- **Only follow modern canning methods that are USDA-approved**

While you may use the same recipes when hosting Christmas or Thanksgiving dinners for your family, make sure that the canning methods you use are the most current ones. Over time, experts may update canning methods and equipment to make them safer. If you plan to make canning a regular thing, keep yourself updated on these methods.

- **Follow the processing times recommended in recipes**

Processing the food in the canning jars is the most important step. Therefore, you should follow the processing times correctly. These processing times (no matter how long) are required to eliminate the undesirable microorganisms in food. Taking shortcuts or extending these times isn't advisable because it could compromise the final product.

- **Practice caution throughout the canning process**

From preparing canned food to storing it, you must practice caution. In particular, transferring the jars after processing must be done carefully, so you don't end up wasting the food, damaging the jars, or injuring yourself. Make sure you have the proper equipment needed for all steps of the process to ensure your safety.

- **Check your canned food before consumption**

Even though you followed all the steps of the process, there is still a chance that the canned food you produce gets spoiled. Therefore, you must check the canned food before consuming it. There are many reasons why canned food gets spoiled, so you shouldn't just open a jar and eat it. Check the smell of the food, the appearance, and even the taste. If everything is okay, that's when you can enjoy the fruits of your labor.

Storage

If you follow the proper canning procedures, you can store your canned food for up to a year after processing. Some recipes will instruct you to do something different, and once you open a jar of food, you will need to make room in the refrigerator and finish the jar as quickly as possible.

As you will notice, the longer you store the food, the softer it becomes, and the more the flavors and colors of the preserved food will fade. So if you want to enjoy the full flavors of the food you have stored, don't wait too long! Here are a few storage tips for you to ensure that the canned food you have stored doesn't get compromised:

- It's recommended to label your canned goods before storing them. On the label, indicate the contents of the jars and the date when you made them. That way, you know which canned foods have been sitting in your storage the longest.

- Make sure that your stored jars are kept in a place with temperatures between 50 to 70 degrees. Also, make sure that your jars aren't placed in direct sunlight. This causes the loss of quality, color, flavor, and nutrients, too.

- If you plan to stack your canning jars, make sure that their vacuum seals remain intact. Also, it's recommended to only stack canning jars two layers high. Then place some kind of solid material between the jars to increase support.
- Don't store your jars in a damp area, as this may cause the seals to start rusting.
- Your storage space should be easy to access so that you can just grab your jars whenever you're hungry or when you need them for cooking.

Knowing how to can your own foods will open you up to a world of possibilities regarding what you eat and how you prepare your meals and snacks. You'll find that it doesn't require a lot of effort, and you can really make some of your food that is full of flavor.

CHAPTER THREE

Canning Tips for Beginners

For many people, the greatest obstacle to canning food is confidence. If you've never done this before, you may doubt your abilities and question whether the food you can will taste good and be safe to eat. You need to put all of that aside and trust yourself. People have been canning food for generations, and it's easier than ever to do it now.

The more you practice canning, the better you get at it. This means that you shouldn't just try it once, especially after purchasing all the basic equipment needed for this practice. These canning tips for beginners should put your mind at ease and help you feel more prepared for the process.

Be Smart with What You Buy

As you have learned, a pressure cooker is a nice instrument to have, especially if you want to work with non-acidic vegetables and meat, but it's not necessary. Instead of spending hundreds of dollars on that, as a beginner, you should be focused on the basics. Invest in some high-quality jars, good lids, and reliable seals. Buy a good set of tongs or a jar lifter. These are the things that matter, and it's where you should initially direct your resources.

When choosing fruits and veggies, opt for those which are just-ripe, not over and not under. For instance, overripe fruits may result in runny jams. This factor can also affect the safety of the final product, so make sure that you choose only the best ingredients for canning.

Label Everything

You may think it's impossible not to remember that you're putting pickled onions in one jar and spicy relish in another. However, you may have these canned goods in your pantry for a year. Don't rely on memory. Label everything. You can write directly on the lids of your jars or use some pretty labels. Write what you've canned and the date it was prepared.

Trust the Recipes

Experimentation is a great idea when throwing together a pasta dish or creating a different way to scramble eggs. However, you don't want to step off the chartered path when canning food. The recipes you find have been tested and tasted, and you can trust that they are safe. Make sure you follow them. Boil the cans for as long as you're told to, and follow every detail. Otherwise, there's no telling what kind of concoction you'll wind up tasting. Remember, the recipes were created specifically for canning. If you end up preparing excessive amounts of ingredients, use them in other dishes instead of trying to incorporate them into your current recipe.

Wipe Those Jars Clean

Once you have filled your jars and you're preparing to process them in the boiling water, make sure you remove any residue or food from the rim. If any substance gets left behind, your jars won't seal. Don't interrupt the vacuum effect that's so important to the canning process.

Jars Are Reusable. Lids Are Not

When you have high-quality jars for canning, you can use them repeatedly. Just make sure you clean them well between eating what's in them and preparing them for new food. Only use jars that are meant for canning. Before using the jars, check for any chips or cracks. If you find any jars that aren't in good shape, don't use them for canning. Also, make sure that the rings of your canning jars aren't rusty or dented, as these will lead to sealing failure.

The lids, however, are not reusable. They should be metal-coated and discarded after you use them. Avoid the plastic lids that have hit the market recently.

These canning tips for beginners will get you started on your canning journey. Allow yourself to make a few mistakes as you get started. As long as you stick with it, everything will come more naturally, and you'll soon be an expert on canning food.

CHAPTER FOUR

Canning Recipes

After learning all of the theoretical information about canning, you can reinforce what you have learned by applying it. To do this, you can start canning different types of foods at home. In this final chapter, we will go through some simple, easy, and delicious canning recipes for you to try. You can start with these recipes to get the feel of the process and then move on to more complex ones after practicing a few times.

Salsas and Sauces

These salsa and sauce products are excellent candidates for canning because they use tomatoes as a base, which provides all the acid you need to safely can your food using the simple boiling water process. There's no need for an expensive processor, and these are hard to screw up. As a beginner, these canning recipes will not only give you great-tasting salsas and sauces, but they'll also prepare you for more complicated recipes.

Spicy Tomato Salsa

Ingredients:
2 pounds fresh tomatoes, peeled and chopped
1 cup red onion, chopped
1 green bell pepper, diced
1 can tomato paste
1 jalapeno pepper, seeded and diced
1 clove garlic, minced
¼ cup white vinegar

2 teaspoons salt
1 teaspoon cayenne pepper
1 teaspoon cumin
3 tablespoons sugar
Juice of 1 lime

Directions:

1. Combine all the ingredients in a pot and cook over low heat for about 2 hours.

2. As soon as the salsa has finished cooking, spoon it into hot jars (you can keep them in simmering water before you fill them). Leave ¼ inch of space at the top and run a spatula or a knife across the top to ensure there are no air bubbles.

3. Wipe the rims of the jars with a damp paper towel and put the rings and lids in place. Lower the jars into a large stockpot of boiling water, ensuring they are covered.

4. Process for 10 minutes and then remove with jar lifters.

5. Leave to cool. Refrigerate after opening.

Zucchini Salsa

Ingredients:
4 onions, chopped
2 green bell peppers, chopped
2 red bell peppers, chopped
10 cups zucchini, peeled and diced
¼ cup pickling salt
2 tablespoons dry mustard
1 tablespoon garlic powder
1 tablespoon cumin
2 cups white vinegar
1 cup brown sugar
1 tablespoon nutmeg
1 tablespoon pepper
1 teaspoon salt
2 tablespoons red pepper flake
5 cups ripe tomatoes, chopped
2 tablespoons cornstarch
12 ounces tomato paste

Directions:
Day One
In a large stockpot, combine zucchini, green pepper, red pepper, pickling salt, and onions. Cover and allow the mixture to stand overnight.

Day Two
1. Rinse the vegetables and drain. Place the mixture into a large stockpot, then add garlic, mustard, cumin, brown sugar, vinegar, nutmeg, pepper, salt, pepper flakes, cornstarch, tomato paste, and tomatoes.

2. Bring the mixture to a boil and allow it to simmer for 15 minutes.

3. Spoon into hot jars and wipe the rims clean. Affix the lids and seals, then process in a boiling water bath for 15 minutes.

4. Remove jars and allow them to cool. Serve chilled.

Spaghetti Sauce

Ingredients:
5 pounds tomatoes, peeled and chopped
1 onion, chopped
1 red bell pepper, chopped
1 stalk celery, chopped
2 carrots, chopped
2 cloves garlic
3 tablespoons brown sugar
2 tablespoons salt
1 tablespoon dried oregano
1 tablespoon dried parsley
1 tablespoon dried basil
1 tablespoon red pepper flakes
2 tablespoons olive oil

Directions:
1. In a large pot, heat the olive oil and add the tomatoes.

2. In a blender or food processor, chop the onion, bell pepper, celery, carrots, and garlic (may need to do 2 or 3 batches).

3. Add the vegetables to the tomatoes and use an immersion blender if you want a smooth sauce. Leave chunky if you prefer.

4. Add the sugar, salt, and spices. Cook on low heat for 3 hours, stirring periodically.

5. Spoon into hot jars, wipe down the rim, and tighten the seal and lid.

6. Process in boiling water for 25 minutes. Remove jars and allow to cool.

Barbeque Sauce

Ingredients:
24 tomatoes, peeled, cored, and chopped
2 cups onion, chopped
2 cups celery, chopped
2 red bell peppers, chopped
2 jalapeno peppers, seeded and chopped
1 green bell pepper, chopped
2 cloves of garlic, minced
1 cup brown sugar
1 tablespoon dry mustard
1 tablespoon paprika
1 teaspoon hot sauce
1 teaspoon cayenne pepper
1¼ cups white vinegar
1 tablespoon canning salt
1 teaspoon black pepper
1 teaspoon white pepper

Directions:
1. In a large pot, combine peppers, onion, tomatoes, celery, and garlic. Cook for 20–30 minutes, until everything gets soft.

2. Use an immersion blender or a food processor to puree. Cook for 30 more minutes.

3. Add salt and pepper and continue cooking over low heat, stirring as it thickens. Add all remaining ingredients and turn off the heat.

4. Spoon into hot jars, leaving ½ inch of headspace at the top. Run a knife or spatula along the top to remove air bubbles and wipe off rims.

5. Place lids and seals in place and process in a boiling water bath for 30 minutes. Remove and cool.

Jams and Relishes

Think about what they once canned "back in the day," and your mind will instantly turn to jams, jellies, and canning recipes like the ones you see here. These are going to taste great, and they have versatile uses. Spread the orange marmalade on your breakfast toast, and use the apple chutney with pork chops.

Apple Pie Jam

Ingredients:
1 cup water
5 cups sugar
½ teaspoon butter
4 large Golden Delicious apples, peeled and sliced
3 ounces liquid fruit pectin
1½ teaspoons ground cinnamon
1 teaspoon ground nutmeg
¼ teaspoon ground mace

Directions:
1. In a Dutch oven, mix the apples and water. Cover and cook over medium heat until the apples are tender.

2. Add butter and sugar, and bring the mixture to a rolling boil over high heat, stirring continuously.

3. Stir in the pectin. Allow the mixture to boil for 1 minute while stirring.

4. Remove the oven from heat and skim off foam. Stir in the spices.

5. Carefully pack the mixture into hot jars, leaving ¼ inch of space at the top.

6. Run a knife or spatula along the top to remove air bubbles.

7. Clean the rims of the jars, and screw on the lids and rings. Process in boiling water for 10 minutes.

8. Remove the jars and cool.

Blueberry & Cinnamon Jam

Ingredients:

⅛ teaspoon ground cloves

¼ teaspoon ground cinnamon

1 tablespoon lemon juice

½ cup liquid fruit protein

3 ½ cups sugar

4 cups blueberries (fresh or frozen)

Directions:

1. Crush the blueberries and place in a saucepan over high heat.

2. Add the lemon juice, cloves, cinnamon, and sugar, then bring to a rolling boil while stirring constantly.

3. Stir the liquid fruit protein into the mixture, then bring to a rolling boil once more. Continue boiling for about 1 minute while stirring constantly.

4. Take the saucepan off the heat and skim the foam off.

5. Use a ladle to transfer the hot mixture into heated canning half-pint jars. Leave ¼ inch of headspace in each jar.

6. Use a bubble remover to get rid of any air bubbles.

7. Wipe the rims of your canning jars, place the lids and rings, and seal them. Check the seals to make sure that they are secure.

8. Process in a boiling water bath for 10 minutes.

9. Use a jar lifter to transfer your canning jars onto a clean surface.

10. Once the bottles have cooled, check the seals again.

11. Label the jars and store them properly.

Peach Mango Jam

Ingredients:
2 pounds peaches, peeled and chopped
2 cups mangoes, peeled and chopped
5 cups sugar
¼ cup lemon juice
3 ounces liquid fruit pectin (half a small pouch)

Directions:
1. Place peaches and lemon juice in a large pot and heat.
2. Crush the peaches with a potato masher until pulpy. Add the mangoes and sugar.
3. As soon as the mixture boils, stir in pectin. Boil for one minute, stirring constantly.
4. Remove from heat. Spoon into hot jars and wipe down the rims.
5. Screw on lids and bands and process in boiling water for 15 minutes. Remove and cool.

Orange Marmalade

Ingredients:

3 pounds oranges

2 lemons

3 cups sugar

Directions:

1. Wash and dry the fruit and peel the skins.

2. Chop the peels. Cover the skins with water and refrigerate overnight.

3. Keep the fruit in sealed containers in the fridge.

4. The next day, coarsely chop the fruit, throwing out seeds.

5. Drain the water from the skins and place in a stockpot. Add the fruit and simmer for 2 hours, stirring occasionally.

6. Add the sugar and cook for 30 minutes more. It will thicken.

7. Place in hot jars, and do a boiling water bath for 20 minutes. Remove to cool.

Apple Chutney

Ingredients:
10 medium apples, peeled, cored, and chopped
1 cup onions, chopped
2 jalapeno peppers, chopped
1 pound raisins
2 cups brown sugar
2 cups white sugar
2 tablespoons ground ginger
2 tablespoons ground cinnamon
2 teaspoons salt
2 cups white vinegar

Directions:
1. Combine everything in a large pot and simmer until thick, for about an hour.

2. Spoon into hot jars, leaving ½ inch at top, and process in a boiling water bath for 20 minutes.

3. Remove from water to cool.

Chocolate Raspberry Jam

Ingredients:
6 pints fresh raspberries
3 squares unsweetened chocolate
4 cups sugar
½ teaspoon butter
2 ounces dry pectin

Directions:
1. In a large pot, crush berries with a potato masher.
2. Chop the chocolate squares into smaller pieces, and add to the berries.
3. In a separate bowl, combine the sugar and the pectin. Once it's combined, add it to the pot and stir continuously.
4. Add the butter and bring the mixture to a boil for 1 minute, stirring.
5. Remove pan from heat and spoon into hot jars, skimming off any foam that is created on top. Wipe down the jars, add the lids and the bands, and process in a boiling water bath for 10 minutes.
6. Remove the jars and cool.

Sweet Pickle Relish

Ingredients:

4 pounds of cucumbers

1 red onion

4 cloves garlic, minced

2 teaspoons dried dill seed

2 teaspoons mustard seed

2 teaspoons celery seed

¼ cup kosher salt

3 cups white vinegar

¾ cup sugar

Directions:

1. Slice the cucumbers lengthwise. Remove seeds. Dice the garlic, cucumber, and onion by hand, or use your food processor.

2. Place all the vegetables in a pot and cover with salt. Allow it to sit for about 2 hours. Stir occasionally. Drain the mixture until all the liquid is released.

3. In a pot over low heat, combine the vinegar, sugar, dill, celery, and mustard. Bring to a boil, and then add the vegetable mixture. Simmer for 15 minutes.

4. Remove from heat and spoon into hot jars. Wipe the rims and settle the lids and bands.

5. Process in a boiling water bath for 10 minutes. Allow to cool.

Fruits and Vegetables

Most of these canning recipes provide enough acidity to be safe with boiling water. Enjoy fruit like cherries and blueberries all year long.

Stewed Tomatoes

Ingredients:
3 pounds fresh tomatoes
1 cup onion, chopped
3 cloves garlic, minced
1 tablespoon dried oregano
1 tablespoon olive oil
1 teaspoon sugar

Directions:
1. Heat the olive oil in a large pot and add the garlic and onion, cooking and stirring for 10 minutes.

2. Add tomatoes, sugar, and oregano and simmer on low heat for 30–45 minutes, until the tomatoes begin softening and breaking down.

3. Spoon the tomatoes into hot glass jars and wipe the rim to remove any food debris.

4. Screw on the tops and the rings and place in a boiling water bath for 20 minutes.

5. Remove the jars and allow to cool.

Canned Blueberries

Ingredients:
8 cups blueberries
2 cups sugar

Directions:
1. Put the berries in a large pot and cover with the sugar. Let them sit just like that for 1 hour.

2. Turn the heat to medium and cook for about 10 minutes, until blueberries begin to release their juices. Once this happens, turn off the heat and spoon the berries into hot jars.

3. Wipe the rims of the jars and screw on the tops and the bands. Place into a boiling water bath for 20 minutes.

4. Remove and cool.

Canned Cherries

Ingredients:

5 pounds of cherries, pitted

3 cups sugar

1 quart water

Directions:

1. In a saucepan, dissolve the sugar in the water. Spoon into hot jars halfway, and add cherries, leaving ½ inch of space at the top.

2. Wipe the rim, tighten the lid, and put the band into place. Process in a boiling water bath for 15 minutes.

3. Remove to cool. If you want to can cherry pie filling, heat the cherries before placing them in the jars.

Crispy Apple Slices

Ingredients:
5 cups apples, sliced into eighths
3¾ cups sugar (¾ cup of sugar per cup of apple slices)

Directions:
1. In a food-grade bucket (5 gallons), layer the apple slices. Scatter them all around, then sprinkle each cup of apple slices with ¾ cup of sugar.

2. After placing all of the apple slices in the bucket, cover it with a plate. Weigh the plate down to press out the juices from the apple slices. Allow to sit for at least 12 hours and up to 24 hours.

3. After squeezing out the juices, pack the apple slices into 1-quart canning jars.

4. Pour the juices into a stockpot and bring to a boil. Once boiling, use a ladle to transfer the juice into the canning jars, making sure that you cover the apple slices completely. Also, make sure that there is ½ inch of space at the top.

5. Run a knife or spatula along the top to remove air bubbles.

6. Wipe the rims of the jars with a damp paper towel and put the rings and lids in place.

7. Process in a boiling water bath for 20 minutes.

8. Leave to cool. Refrigerate after opening.

Pickled Beets

Ingredients:
6 cups vinegar
2 cups water
4 cups sugar
1 tablespoon ground cinnamon
¾ tablespoon salt
½ tablespoon ground cloves
6 pounds beets, peeled and sliced

Directions:
1. In a heavy stockpot, combine the sugar, white vinegar, cinnamon, water, cloves, and salt. Bring to a boil, and stir until the sugar has dissolved completely.

2. Pack the beets into sterilized jars and cover with the pickling solution, leaving ¼ inch of space at the top.

3. Wipe rims, affix lids and bands, and process in a boiling water bath for 30 minutes.

4. Allow to cool. Refrigerate after opening.

Dill Pickles

Ingredients:
6 medium cucumbers
3 cups water
¼ cup pickling salt
2 cups white vinegar
Sprigs of fresh dill
1 head garlic, peeled and cloves separated

Directions:
1. Slice cucumbers twice lengthwise. Set aside.

2. In a pot, combine water, pickling salt, and vinegar. Bring to a boil for about 10 minutes.

3. Place the cucumbers in hot jars, and add the brining solution to the jars, leaving ½ inch space at the top.

4. Add fresh dill and cloves of garlic to take up some space around the cucumbers.

5. Process in a boiling water bath for 15 minutes, and remove to cool.

Martini Green Beans

Ingredients:

3 cups vinegar

2 cups water

¼ cup kosher salt

¼ cup sugar

16 cups green beans, trimmed, sliced, and boiled for 5 minutes

8 cloves of garlic

5 cups onions, sliced

1 teaspoon peppercorn

1 teaspoon mustard seed

4 bay leaves

4 chili peppers

8 juniper berries

1 cup gin

8 lemon peel strips

1 tablespoon dill weed, chopped

1 tablespoon dill seed

Directions:

1. Sterilize 4 canning jars as well as lids in boiling water.

2. In a large stockpot, combine the water, sugar, salt, and vinegar. Bring the mixture to a boil.

3. Add the beans and onions, cover the pot, and simmer for 15 minutes.

4. To each jar, add 2 cloves of garlic cloves, 1 bay leaves, 1 chili pepper, ¼ teaspoon peppercorn, ¼ teaspoon mustard seed, ¼ tablespoon dill weed, ¼ tablespoon dill seed, 2 juniper berries, and 2 lemon zest strips. Pour ¼ cup gin into every jar.

5. Pack the onions and beans into each jar and cover with the liquid, leaving ¼ inch of space at the top.

6. Run a knife or spatula along the top to remove air bubbles.

7. Clean the rims of the jars, and screw on the lids and rings. Process in boiling water for 10–15 minutes.

8. Cool and store in a dark, cool place for up to 2 to 3 weeks. Serve chilled.

Curry Cauliflower

Ingredients:
3 pounds fresh cauliflower
1 cup vinegar
2 cups water
2 teaspoons salt, plus another 3 teaspoons salt
1/3 cup sugar
3 bay leaves
½ teaspoon turmeric
2 teaspoons curry powder
1 teaspoon crushed red pepper

Directions:
1. Combine water, vinegar, 2 teaspoons salt, and sugar in a saucepan. Simmer and stir until the sugar has dissolved and everything is combined. Remove the pan from heat.

2. Wash the cauliflower and pull the florets into small pieces. Toss it with the 3 teaspoons salt, and leave it to sit so the moisture can be released.

3. Drain the excess fluid. Add the bay leaves, turmeric, curry powder, and red pepper to the cauliflower.

4. Press cauliflower mixture into hot jars, and use tongs or a spatula to press everything down. Add the liquid on top, leaving ½ inch at the top.

5. Clean the rims of the jars, and screw on the lids and rings. Process in a boiling water bath for 10 minutes.

6. Remove and cool.

Red Pepper Marmalade

Ingredients:

¾ cup lemon juice

8 large red bell peppers

¼ cup orange juice

¼ cup red wine vinegar

2 cups sugar

2 tablespoons tomato paste

4 garlic cloves, peeled and chopped

1 onion, peeled and finely chopped

½ teaspoon salt

½ teaspoon cayenne pepper

1 teaspoon fresh marjoram, chopped

1 teaspoon fresh rosemary, chopped

1 zest of lemon

1 zest of orange

Directions:

1. Half the red bell peppers and remove the core and seeds. Grill the peppers until slightly charred.

2. Finely chop 6 of the red peppers and slice the remaining 2.

3. In a saucepan, combine all the ingredients and stir over low heat until all the sugar has dissolved.

4. Bring the mixture to a boil and simmer for 10 minutes, until the mixture thickens.

5. Remove pan from heat and spoon into hot jars, skimming off any foam that is created on top. Wipe down the jars, add the lids and the bands, and process in a boiling water bath for 15 minutes.

6. Remove the jars and cool.

Fresh Corn

Ingredients:
32 pounds corn (in-husk)
7 teaspoons canning salt (non-iodized, 1 tsp per quart)

Directions:
1. Remove the silk and husk from each of the corn cobs. For the silk, you can use a soft vegetable brush. For the kernels, you can use a knife to remove them from the cob.

2. Fill 1-quart canning jars with the corn kernels. Leave 1 inch of headspace since corn tends to expand when cooked.

3. Pour boiling water into the jars just enough to completely cover the corn kernels.

4. Use a bubble remover to get rid of any air bubbles. Make sure that there is still 1 inch of headspace at the top.

5. Add 1 teaspoon of salt to each of the canning jars.

6. Wipe the rims of your canning jars, place the lids and rings, and seal them. Check the seals to make sure that they are secure.

7. Process the 1-quart jars for 1 hour and 25 minutes in your pressure canner. Read the instructions for your canner and follow them.

8. After processing, use a jar lifter to transfer your canning jars onto a clean surface.

9. Once the jars have cooled, check the seals again. After checking, label the jars and store them properly.

Meat and Fish

With meat, you'll need to upgrade from the general boiling water bath to a serious piece of kitchen equipment—the pressure canner. This will keep your food safe and free from bacteria.

Canned Venison

Ingredients:
Fresh venison meat
Canning salt

Directions:
1. Preheat your pressure canner. Slice your meat across the grain into strips or chunks of whatever size you prefer.

2. Pack the meat into hot jars, leaving about 1 inch at the top. Add 1 tablespoon of canning salt per quart that your jar holds. So, if you're packing meat into a 4-quart jar, you'll add 4 tablespoons of salt.

3. Use a spatula or the back of a spoon to force out air bubbles before you screw the lid on and affix the band.

4. Place your jars in the pressure canner and make sure there's at least 1 inch of space between them. They shouldn't touch one another.

5. Process in your canner for an hour and a half. Remove your jars and allow them to cool.

Canned Roast Beef

Ingredients:
3 pounds chuck roast, cubed
1 large onion, cut into eighths
1½ teaspoons salt

Directions:
1. Preheat your pressure canner.

2. Pack the meat into 4 hot jars, add the onion to each of the jars, followed by ½ teaspoon salt per pound of meat, leaving about 1 inch of space at the top.

3. Use a spatula or the back of a spoon to force out air bubbles before you screw the lid on and affix the band.

4. Place the jars in the pressure canner and process for an hour and a half. Remove the jars and allow them to cool.

Canned Fish

Ingredients:
5 pounds trout, pike, or any whitefish
White vinegar (1 tablespoon per jar used)
Tomato soup (1 tablespoon per jar used)
Salt (1 teaspoon per jar used)

Directions:
1. Clean and scale the fish. Remove head, tail, fins, scales, and entrails. Cut fish into 2 or 3-inch chunks or strips, depending on your preference.

2. Spoon into hot jars, leaving at least 1 inch of space at the top. Add the salt, tomato soup, and vinegar to each jar before sealing the lids.

3. Place in your pressure canner and process for 1 hour.

4. Use a jar lifter to transfer your canning jars onto a clean surface.

5. Once the jars have cooled, check the seals again.

6. Label the jars and store them properly.

Smoked Fish

Ingredients:

Fish (lightly smoked, partially cooked)

Directions:

1. Cut the fish into pieces the same length as your canning pints.

2. Pack the fish slices into canning pints with 1-inch of headspace.

3. Wipe the rims of your canning pints, place the lids and rings, and seal them. Check the seals to make sure that they are secure.

4. Place the pints in the pressure canner and process for 1 hour and 50 minutes.

5. After processing, use a jar lifter to transfer your canning pints onto a clean surface.

6. Once the jars have cooled, check the seals again.

7. Label the pints and store them properly.

Canned Chicken Soup

Ingredients:
6 quarts chicken broth
6 cups cooked chicken
2 cups celery, chopped
2 cups carrots, chopped
1 cup onions, chopped
1 cup mushrooms, sliced
2 cloves garlic
1 tablespoon salt
1 teaspoon pepper

Directions:
1. In a large stockpot, heat the broth and the chicken.
2. Add the celery, carrots, onions, mushrooms, and garlic. Bring the mixture to a boil. Add the salt and pepper.
3. Use a slotted spoon to grab the solid parts of the soup and place into hot jars. Add the cooking liquid on top, and leave about 1 inch of space at the top of the jars.
4. Place lids and bands on the jars and process in your pressure canner for an hour and a half.
5. Remove and allow jars to cool.

Bone Broth

Ingredients:

½ cup garlic, minced

1 cup leeks or shallots, chopped

1 cup onions, chopped

2 cups carrots, chopped

4 cups bone broth (homemade or store-bought)

4 pounds meaty beef soup bones

Salt and pepper to taste

Directions:

1. In a stockpot, combine all of the ingredients. Then fill the pot with water, leaving a headspace of about 2 inches at the top.

2. Bring the mixture to a boil over medium heat.

3. Once boiling, reduce the heat to low and allow to simmer for a minimum of 4 hours.

4. Pour the bone broth through a strainer to remove all of the solid bits.

5. If you don't want your bone broth to be excessively fatty, cool it down completely, then skim the fat. However, the extra fat does add to the richness and flavor of the broth, so you may skip this step.

6. Right before canning, bring the strained bone broth to a boil in a stockpot once again.

7. As you bring the water in your pressure canner to a boil, use a ladle to transfer the hot bone broth into canning jars with 1 inch of headspace.

8. Wipe the rims of your canning jars, place the lids and rings, and seal them. Check the seals to make sure that they are secure.

9. Place the jars in the pressure canner and process for 25 minutes.

10. Turn the heat off and allow your pressure canner to cool

down to room temperature on its own. This may take up to an hour.

11. Once completely cool, use a jar lifter to transfer your canning jars onto a clean surface.

12. Check the seals again, label the jars, and store them properly.

Conclusion

There you have it!

All of the fundamental information you need to know about canning. With everything you have learned in this book, you can now start canning your own food at home. Start with the simple recipes in the last chapter, and the more you get the hang of the process, the easier it becomes. Canning isn't only beneficial, but it's also fun to do. Soon, you can start experimenting with different types of food to make things more interesting for you and your whole family.

Now that you know how to can foods properly, you can have any kind of food items and even meals available to you throughout the year. Gone are the days when you had to wait for seasons to come so that you could satisfy your cravings. Happy canning!

Finally, I want to thank you for reading my book. If you enjoyed the book, please share your thoughts and post a review on the book retailer's website. It would be greatly appreciated!

Best wishes,

Melanie Bennet

CPSIA information can be obtained
at www.ICGtesting.com
Printed in the USA
LVHW080419020822
724967LV00017B/206

9 798201 927714